The Fabian Society

The Fabian Society has played a central ro
development of political ideas and public
the key challenges facing the UK and the
changing society and global economy, the
explore the political ideas and the policy reforms which will define progressive
politics in the new century.

The Society is unique among think tanks in being a democratically-constituted
membership organisation. It is affiliated to the Labour Party but is editorially
and organisationally independent. Through its publications, seminars and
conferences, the Society provides an arena for open-minded public debate.

GW01464174

Fabian Society
11 Dartmouth Street
London SW1H 9BN
www.fabian-society.org.uk

Fabian ideas
Editor: Adrian Harvey
Design: Rory Fisher

First published March 2002

ISBN 0 7163 0601 8
ISSN 1469 0136

British Library Cataloguing in Publication data.
A catalogue record for this book is available from the British Library.

Printed by Bell & Bain Limited, Glasgow

Contents

About the authors

Janet Bush is Director of New Europe. She is a former journalist at Reuters, The *Financial Times*, the BBC and *The Times*, where she was Economics Correspondent and then Economics Editor. She was named Young Financial Journalist of the Year in 1987. She is a member of the Labour Party.

Larry Elliott is Economics Editor of The *Guardian*, where he has worked since 1988. He has been a member of the Labour Party—a brief period in the mid-90s apart—since 1974. He is a visiting research fellow of the University of Hertfordshire. With Dan Atkinson, he is co-author of *The Age of Insecurity* (Verso).

Andrew Gamble is Professor of Politics and Director of the Political Economy Research Centre at the University of Sheffield. He is co-editor of The *Political Quarterly* and *New Political Economy* and a Fellow of the British Academy. His books include *The Free Economy and the Strong State* (Palgrave) and *Politics and Fate* (Polity).

Acknowledgements

Andrew Gamble would like to thank Stephen George, Adrian Harvey, Michael Jacobs, Gavin Kelly, Michael Kenny, David Marquand and Ben Rosamond for their comments and advice on earlier drafts.

66

Foreword

Michael Jacobs
General Secretary, Fabian Society

There's something puzzling about the euro debate. The European single currency has been on the table for nearly a decade now. The subject has been the cause of bitter division in one of the two major British political parties for at least half of that period, and sometimes ill-concealed differences between leading ministers in the government for nearly as long. Most of our newspapers are fiercely pro or (in the main) anti, as their often nakedly partisan coverage makes plain. And yet how many British citizens could honestly say that they properly understand the issues involved, or have yet formed a considered view?

This will no doubt all change, of course, when a referendum is eventually called. Contrary to fevered speculation this could yet be some years away. But even if it is, there is no reason why we should not have a proper debate on the merits of British entry now. The media often behave as if such a debate cannot happen until the Prime Minister tells us we can have it. This is ridiculous: we are grown up citizens, and we do not need permission to discuss one of the most serious issues facing the country over the coming decade.

Three things must immediately be said about such a debate. First, it is not the same one as we had a few years ago. Then the question was whether the single currency was a good idea. The

UK was having the same debate as the rest of Europe. But now it exists. The question has changed; it is whether or not we should join it. And so this becomes a specifically British debate. It inevitably concerns our relationships with our European partners; and it must take place not in the abstract but in the real world in which the rest of Europe has adopted, and is now using, the single currency.

Second, any attempt to argue for entry on the grounds that it is 'inevitable' is specious, and will surely prove counter-productive. For there is going to be a referendum, which means that it is patently not inevitable at all.

Third, it is not just a question of economics. The idea that all this is really just a technical matter of the five economic tests which the government has set out, and once they're decided the issue is settled, cannot be right. The economics are indeed crucial: few people argue either for or against entry irrespective of the impact on the British economy. In particular, the tests are vital to determine the timing and exchange rate at which the UK might join. These will in turn have a profound effect on how the single currency will impact on the UK: it can be a perfectly coherent position to be in favour of joining at one exchange rate and time but against joining at others.

But the economic arguments are not sufficient on their own. Adoption of a single currency is a constitutional change: it relocates sovereignty over monetary policy, and therefore over economic policy more widely. The acts both of joining and of not joining would significantly alter our relations with the rest of the European Union. And in turn both would inevitably mean a significant shift in the sense and nature of British identity.

This pamphlet is therefore an attempt to conduct a debate about the politics as well as the economics of euro entry. It does so from the left of the political spectrum. Although they have fundamentally opposed views, the two essays here have similar starting points. They are concerned with the effect which joining or not joining the euro will have on the chances of promoting social democratic goals—full employment, the provision of high quality public services, employee rights, environmental protection. Both place their analysis in the context of globalisation and the recent development of international capitalism. And both acknowledge the importance to the euro debate of the wider constitutional options facing the European Union.

Proponents of political arguments often try to suggest that their own side is 100 per cent right and their opponents are talking complete nonsense. But in reality political differences are rarely like this, and this is particularly so on the question of euro entry. There are strong arguments on both sides—and considerable uncertainties too. It is hoped that this pamphlet will help readers judge the balance.

It is particularly important that Labour Party members should get the chance to do so. For in the hurly burly of party politics an important truth can easily be lost. This is that to make up your mind about a political issue you need to hear both sides of the argument. This matters especially in the case of the euro, because, whenever the referendum is called, the Labour Government is going to be in favour of entry. Since its reputation will be on the line, there will understandably be a lot of pressure for Labour Party members to support the Government. But the Government cannot rely on loyalty alone, because in the end Labour Party members will have a secret ballot in the referendum just like every other citizen. And to make up their minds they will have to consider both the case for entry and the case against. Ultimately, therefore, even party and campaign managers should welcome a genuine debate.

It is to help such a debate that the Fabian Society is publishing this pamphlet. I hope it does so.

“

1 | **For** Andrew Gamble

Arguments for and against the euro in Britain have generally focused on economic issues. The impression is given
that nothing else is at stake, and that all that counts are the
five economic tests and whether or not they can be said to have
been satisfied. Opponents of the euro often complain bitterly
about this, arguing that the political consequences of joining are
far more important than any short run economic consequences.
Even if the economic judgement were overwhelmingly
favourable (which of course they deny it could ever be) they
would still oppose entry on political and constitutional grounds.

Joining the euro, they claim, would be an irreversible and
therefore unacceptable surrender of sovereignty. The reply of
many of those in favour of joining is that the decision has nothing
to do with sovereignty; it really is only about economics and a
utilitarian calculation of short-term costs and benefits. This is a
mistake. Sovereignty is at the very heart of the matter, and
should be made central to the argument for joining the euro.
There are very strong economic arguments for Britain being in
the euro but the economic case by itself will never be conclusive
or decisive. It is the political choice that counts.

Sovereignty and the global economy

To make this political case, the euro needs placing in a much
wider framework than is often done in Britain. The world has

changed in the last thirty years. The global economy has become more interconnected and more open, the bipolar international system of the cold war has collapsed, and neo-liberalism has become the ruling orthodoxy in international and domestic politics. Power has shifted within global capitalism away from national governments towards transnational agents and networks, in particular transnational companies and financial markets.

The institutions of the emerging global economy and global polity increasingly shape domestic choices. Nation-states by themselves can exercise little effective sovereignty within this new world order. If they are to avoid competitive deregulation and preserve the social democratic gains of the second half of the twentieth century, they need to come together to establish new democratic forms of cooperation. The European Union is the best contemporary example. It is the region where social democratic values and the political will to uphold them are strongest; it has emerged as the major counterweight to the United States in the global economy; and it has developed much stronger regulatory powers than those found in other regional groupings such as NAFTA or global bodies such as the UN.

The argument for the euro is therefore a political argument about globalisation: how we should respond to it, and how we can avoid experiencing it as a malign fate over which we have no control. This does not mean abandoning national democracy or nation-states or national economies; on the contrary they are the foundations on which any international structure has to be built. But we cannot rely on them alone. We have to extend democracy and co-operation and solidarity beyond the national level.

Sovereignty confers the authority to make binding decisions, but it also signifies the capacity to act and to make choices. There is little point in enjoying formal sovereignty if real sovereignty resides elsewhere. The argument about the euro is this kind of argument. Will joining it enhance or diminish our ability to control the things that matter? Will it strengthen our democracy or will it weaken it? The euro is an acknowledgement of the increasing interdependence that now exists between national economies in Europe and the resulting advantages that come from greater cooperation in a competitive global economy. Trying to ensure the conditions for macroeconomic stability in one country no longer makes very good sense; the room for genuine autonomy and genuine flexibility was never high, but it has shrunk further in the last thirty years. The value of having a stable macroeconomic framework, a common currency, a single market, low interest rates and low inflation are often described as part of a neo-liberal consensus; but they are also the preconditions for any serious attempt to realise substantive social democratic goals, including redistribution of income and assets, environmental protection, and high quality universal public services.

The question we need to ask is: how can self-government be best secured in the present global economy? National governments are handicapped in achieving their central aims if they are not prepared to pool sovereignty and create new forms of transnational authority and new kinds of institutions and transnational political spaces. The European Union is currently the world's most prominent and developed example of this trend. What this implies is that national sovereignty has to be unpacked and rethought. It is not something which adheres mystically to nation-states and only nation-states. It is the capacity to act. As such, it is a feature of jurisdictions. But contrary to myth, jurisdictions have rarely conformed simply to the model of a set of self-contained and self-sufficient, inward-looking, tightly defined and exclusive national territories. The international system was always more complex than this and in our world it has become still more so. Jurisdictions increasingly overlap, which means that effective sovereignty (and therefore effective self-government) often requires formal sovereignty to be transferred from nation-states and pooled, by creating some form of transnational authority.

The economic benefits from a successful euro will be stable prices and a stable exchange rate, which then makes it possible to sustain higher levels of employment, public spending and redistribution than would otherwise be possible. Crises in the financial markets in the past have wrecked the programmes of social democratic governments in Europe—Britain in 1976, France in 1981, Sweden in 1994; national economic sovereignty was no protection. Major currency fluctuations are immensely damaging (between 1979 and 1981 sterling climbed 30 per cent against the German Mark and unemployment trebled to 3 million). They cannot be eliminated entirely, but joining the euro is the best way of minimising them, since 8 out of 10 of Britain's trading partners are members of the eurozone, accounting for well over half of Britain's trade. Within a few years there may be as many as twenty-five members of the EU, all of them using the euro. If Denmark and Sweden vote, as expected, to join in 2003, Britain will be the only member of the EU left outside. The euro will become increasingly important for the UK economy as British firms start trading in it in order to compete in the single market and the longer Britain stays out, the higher the penalty is likely to become in terms of lost inward investment, as well as higher transaction costs.

There is nothing inevitable about Britain joining the euro and, as Janet Bush and Larry Elliott point out, you do not have to be against Britain's membership of the European Union to be against the euro. The case still has to be made on its merits, above all its political merits. Part of that case though is that in the future it will become increasingly difficult for Britain to play a full part in the EU while remaining outside the euro. The question facing Britain is no longer whether a single currency is a good idea as an abstract possibility. That debate lies in the past. The single currency exists; the question now is whether Britain should join it.

One of the most important things to grasp about the euro, as indeed about the whole process of European integration, is that this is not a single process with a single destination, but a complex experiment which opens up very different possibilities and alternatives, which are rightly the subject of political choices and wide-ranging debate in all European countries. There is not one pre-ordained future. The euro has a potential for harm as well as for good. It could, as Bush & Elliott suggest, severely limit the prospects for social democracy in Europe. But it could also dramatically extend them.

A neo-liberal Europe?

There is no shortage of pessimists keeping Bush & Elliott company in proclaiming the dire consequences of adopting the euro. They paint a scenario of almost unrelieved gloom, and are particularly bleak about the damage that the euro will do to the left across Europe. But a little optimism is in order. We should lift up our eyes and realise the ways in which a successful euro can enhance not diminish the prospects for the causes and programmes of the left in Europe, by making it easier for left of centre policies to be pursued by national governments and by the European Union. This optimistic scenario for the euro underpins the political case for joining. This is not to suggest that everything in this scenario will happen. There is after all a strong right of centre argument for the euro as well. The European Union is not on a single track and its political character and direction are not pre-ordained. But that is no reason for abandoning the euro entirely to the right, as Bush & Elliott would have us do. If Britain under a Labour Government votes to join the euro the chances of the optimistic scenario being realised will be greatly enhanced. We can affect the outcome by what we do.

One of the main arguments used against the euro is that joining a common currency removes one of the most important symbols of national sovereignty, and with it one of the most crucial powers which makes self-government possible. The eurosceptic right complains that creating a single currency is a major step towards a federal or even a unitary superstate which will end by extinguishing all national sovereignties and transferring all powers away from nation-states to a new executive in Brussels. The complaint from the eurosceptic left, as set out by Bush & Elliott in this pamphlet, is rather different; they would not object to the euro if there was any prospect of a democratically account- able European state, because such a state might then pursue social democratic policies at the European level. But they argue that there is no real prospect of such a state. Instead they see the euro as part of a neo-liberal project, one aimed at insulating deci- sion-making on crucial economic questions from any democratic accountability or participation. Montagu Norman, Governor of the Bank of England in the interwar years, wanted to make the management of currencies 'politician proof', and a similar ambi- tion is attributed by contemporary critics to the architects of the euro. They attack the creation of supranational institutions like the European Central Bank because they are not accountable and because they entrench neo-liberal macro-economic policies that national governments cannot alter. If social democratic govern- ments are elected within any member state of the eurozone, they will be powerless to implement the policies on which they were elected, because they cannot change this external framework.

The loss of economic sovereignty which the euro entails is the driving force in the pessimistic scenario of the eurosceptics. Each member state, whatever the complexion of its government, must accept passively in its own national territory the effects on unem- ployment, inflation and growth which are the outcome of the monetary policies being pursued by the European Central Bank.

The result, it is argued, will be huge unevenness of economic performance in different regions in the eurozone and a sharp polarisation of income and wealth, of growth rates, and of levels of unemployment. This in turn will set up a competitive race to the bottom, in which the unsuccessful regions will be forced to lower their costs in order to compete, and they will do this by reducing wages, removing employment protection, and cutting universal services. The logic of this pessimistic scenario is that the only way to avoid the rigours of neo-liberal economic policies is to retain national economic sovereignty, and in particular control over the national currency. Social democratic economic policy can only be national economic policy, which means that social democracy is indissolubly tied to national economies and to nation-states; social democracy in one country.

What the pessimistic scenario fails to explain is why European integration, which at every stage has depended on the agreement of the member states, should have proceeded as far as it has. Why should national governments and national electorates have been so ready to cede their vital powers? Why is there no major political party in any part of the Union (even Britain) openly campaigning for withdrawal from the Union? And why have all mainstream centre left parties in the rest of Europe been enthusiastic supporters of the drive to the single currency? The answer is fairly obvious. It lies in the tangible benefits that being part of such a Union confers on its members. The increase in collective sovereignty makes it easier, not more difficult, for states to achieve their national goals.

In the new global economy, national economic sovereignty is an illusion. The case for the euro can therefore be made simply in terms of national self-interest. But, though vital, this is in fact too limited a perspective. We need to look at the broader political questions which European integration inevitably raises. One of the advantages of the euro from this standpoint is that it forces into the open questions about the constitutional architecture of Europe and makes it much harder for these to be avoided in the way, up to now, they often have been.

A self-governing Europe

The optimistic left of centre scenario for the euro starts from this fact. The EU is a new kind of polity. It will never be a centralised nation-state. How could it be? There is no European nation, no European consciousness, no European identity of the kind that would be necessary to provide the basis for legitimate state authority. The EU is something altogether more interesting. It is a new form of political authority and therefore a new kind of political space created by political agreement to pool sovereignty, so transferring certain functions to European agencies, while others remain firmly in the hands of nation-states. A single currency does not mean a single government. The question as to which state functions should be discharged at the European level, which at national level and which at sub-national level are being decided pragmatically. There is a fierce debate around these questions in all European countries; the balance has changed in the past and will no doubt change again in the future. That is in the nature of the kind of supranational, or as some prefer post-national, authority which the EU has become. It is not in transition to a new unitary or federal state, but neither is it at all likely to move back to a loose association of sovereign nation-states.

The introduction of the euro changes the balance by transferring a major new policy competence, monetary policy, to the European level. Its consequences will be far-reaching because of the many incremental changes and adjustments which will follow. By consolidating the European economy as a single market it brings other policy issues into focus for the EU, and reshapes its agenda. In particular it highlights the need for policies to make the movement of labour easier within the EU and to enlarge the budget, so as to make possible much larger redistributions of resources between different parts of the eurozone than are possible at the moment, in order to correct imbalances in levels of employment which can no longer be corrected through the adjustment of exchange rates.

Whether the EU develops such policies will be a crucial test of its ability to make the euro work. So too will be the creation of new ways to allow Europe's politicians to set the framework within which the European Central Bank operates, in particular the targets for inflation it seeks to meet, its attitude to growth and employment, and the Growth and Stability Pact. Pessimists argue, as do Bush & Elliott, that nothing will change. The neo-liberal character of economic and monetary union is set in concrete. But while optimists agree that there is no certainty that the right policies will be adopted, since they will have to be agreed by the member states, they argue that the practical necessity of new policies and new institutional arrangements will become ever more obvious now that the euro has been successfully established. The experience of using the euro will itself create a momentum for change in other policies, in order to make sure that the euro succeeds.

From this standpoint therefore the euro is not just a technical economic matter but the start of a new process in the development of policies and institutions which will enhance the self-government of all the participating member states, through their decision to pool their sovereignty over monetary policy. The creation of long-term macrostability in the eurozone area will increase not diminish their ability to manage their domestic national economies and provide the services and living standards their peoples want.

The euro is a political creation, and the institutions which govern it are not a fixed and final political settlement; many changes are going to be necessary in the years ahead, and there will be different views as to what those should be. The political agenda in Europe will shift as national and European elections alter the balance of political regimes in different nation-states as well as the party make-up of the European Parliament. No party has a natural majority in Europe; recently the centre-left has been dominant at the national level and therefore in the Council of Ministers, but it will not always be, and indeed at present the electoral tide in Europe appears to be flowing against the left. It has already lost the majority it held in the European Parliament. Institutions like the euro, however, will outlast short-term political changes. Almost all of Europe's major political parties are committed to it, and there are certainly very few on the left anywhere in Europe who think that reasserting national sovereignty and abandoning the euro is the way ahead. Instead the mainstream European left sees the advent of the euro as an opportunity for pressing the case for reforms in European institutions and changes in European policies which will help promote a wider social democratic agenda.

The issue for the left is whether a common currency at the EU level is an important condition for achieving these goals or not. It is obviously a political question. Britain is already a currency union, formed at the time of the Act of Union between England and Scotland in 1707. A common currency and a single market have been promoted for the whole of Britain because there were both political as well as economic advantages which flowed from treating the UK as a single and undivided economic space. It established a politics concerned with the desirability of making transfers between different parts of this economic space and facilitating the movement of labour and other resources around it, as well as providing universal public services for all the citizens within it and formulating general rules for regulating it. Out of this politics emerged the British left and the British labour movement, which helped transform British politics and the British economy generally for the better over the last hundred years.

Europe now offers the same opportunity. The British Labour Party was at first slow to grasp its potential, and has at times been strongly opposed to membership of the European Community. As recently as 1983 the party manifesto advocated withdrawal from the European Community altogether, arguing that EC rules would obstruct the kind of national protectionist economic programme Labour regarded essential at that time to put the British economy back on its feet. But in the last twenty years Labour has come to accept what every other centre-left party in Europe had already concluded; that the cause of social democracy is helped not hindered through membership of the European Union. This is not just because it has defused nationalist tensions and traditional rivalries and enmities within Europe. It is because it has provided the framework underpinning the economic stability and prosperity which the rest of the Community has enjoyed for so long—establishing a common regulatory space in which labour, social and environmental standards have all been raised.

The euro raises questions about the forms as well as the substance of self-government. As already indicated, the EU is constantly evolving. It is a political and economic experiment, which constantly throws up new problems, new dilemmas, and new opportunities. The euro should be liberating for the left because it allows us to think of how problems which can no longer be satisfactorily tackled at the national level might be addressed at the European level. But it is not all one way. By encouraging clearer thinking about Europe as a political and economic space, it may also help to highlight the need to transfer some policies from the European level back to local or national jurisdictions. Agriculture, for example, may well now move in this direction.

The campaigns for constitutional reform of the UK in the last few decades persuaded a majority on the left that the system of government in Britain had become overcentralised and no longer well adapted to the realisation of social democratic objectives. A measure of devolution has been achieved since 1997, and has begun to move Britain towards a federal structure in which the responsibility for different policies is located at different levels of the state. At the same time Britain is part of a parallel process in the European Union, which has acquired new impetus with the current discussions on the right constitutional framework for Europe, as reflected in the debate on the future of Europe (http://europa.eu.int/futurum/index_en.htm), the European Commission's White Paper on European Governance, and the establishment of a Constitutional Convention chaired by Giscard d'Estaing.

The debate on the future of Europe has raised the question of whether Europe should be a federated United States of Europe, or a federation of nation-states, or a Union with federal powers. This has set alarm bells ringing again in Britain, where federalism has long been a grossly misused and misunderstood term. Yet as has been repeated so often, what it properly signifies is not centralisation, as in the notion of a superstate, but decentralisation through a division of powers, and the precise articulation of the powers and competencies of different levels of political authority. A federal, or more accurately a confederal, constitution for Europe (one based firmly on nation-states), would actually, contrary to what Eurosceptics often claim, protect state rights by specifying them, and making it much harder than it is at the moment for European institutions and agencies to encroach upon them.

Once the range of opinion within Europe on the appropriate constitutional framework for this new kind of polity is appreciated, then it is obvious that joining the euro is not the death warrant for national democracy which Bush & Elliott make it out to be; it does not entail that a centralised, unitary European state is round the corner, or that an undemocratic authoritarian regime of Brussels officials and European central bankers is about to supplant the democratic rights of elected national Parliaments to supervise and to change their country's monetary policy. On the contrary. The existence of the euro makes it easier to reassess where powers should be located and to reallocate them between levels. It makes it easier to bring about a Europe of the Regions as well as a Europe of nation-states, a multi-level polity with multi-level governance. It will also help focus attention on the reforms that need to be undertaken to ensure that the European Central Bank and similar agencies are not only accountable through the Council of Ministers, but also in other more open and transparent ways. In all these ways it can be expected to enhance rather than diminish the capacity of the British and all other members of the eurozone to govern themselves.

A social democratic Europe

Making it easier to govern ourselves and choose the things we want by pooling our sovereignty with others is at the heart of the case for the euro. Once the euro is seen in this way other consequences follow. Establishing the euro creates a need for additional common policies to ensure that it works smoothly for all regions in the eurozone. But it will be a catalyst for change in other areas also—for redistribution, for regulation, for trade unions and associations, and for citizens.

It is crucial to recognise how the existence of the euro assists the promotion of key social democratic agendas. In particular, for regulating capitalism in ways that promote greater social justice and environmental protection. The single currency will increase the cohesion of the Union and make it easier to argue for the creation of new policy capacities and responsibilities at the

European level and for existing ones to be strengthened and deepened. As most social democrats have long recognised, the traditional goals of social democracy cannot be pursued in isolation. There needs to be transnational co-operation if they are to be achieved. This is so in two senses. European co-operation to create macroeconomic stability and foster trade helps each member state realise the social democratic goals of providing high quality, universal public services. It also makes Europe better placed to influence the way in which the global economy is regulated. The argument for tougher and more effective regulation still has to be won, but the advent of the euro makes it that much easier for the case to be heard. It puts new issues on the agenda because the existence of the eurozone compels Europe to think in terms of common policies and common responses. The decision to pool sovereignty which the euro represents cannot be insulated from other issues. Europe will be forced to confront them, and it is vital that the UK is part of this process.

The most successful social democratic regimes in Europe in the last forty years have succeeded in combining economic efficiency and social justice, and they have done this by identifying the services which need to be provided collectively, and the framework of rules and institutions which should govern the operation of markets. But many of the problems confronting social democracy today require the creation of political capacities and competences beyond the level of the nation-state. Whether the issue is effective environmental regulation, or macroeconomic stability, or higher labour standards, or global poverty, the need for national governments to co-operate in establishing strong transnational authorities which can set international standards is plain. The level of interdependence between the national economies of Europe is now so great that the framing of common policies and common standards makes obvious sense.

The euro can assist in this. But there is a further argument as well. One of the greatest needs within the global economy is that there should be a more effective championing of environmental and redistributive issues, whether environmental treaties and agreements like Kyoto, debt relief, increasing aid budgets, fair trade, or reform of the IMF and the World Bank. The present unchallenged United States hegemony carries many dangers, not least the lack of interest of the present US administration in promoting genuine multilateral forms of transnational governance, rather than forms of governance which one-sidedly protect and advance US interests. The establishment of the euro makes the EU an increasingly important counterweight to the Americans, not as a rival military superpower, but as an alternative model for governance and regulation of the global economy, and a pole of influence around which other countries can gather.

If the EU had remained a loose association of states, its potential influence would be far less. It is the growing cohesion of Europe and its ability to formulate common policies on key issues such as environmental protection which makes the establishment of the euro such a significant and a symbolic step. It both underlines and underpins the common purpose which Europe has come to represent. This is often misunderstood. To wield effective influence in the way the global economy is governed the last thing that is needed is for Europe to become a conventional superpower, with all the usual trappings of statehood, and all the attendant dangers of great power rivalry. That would move the world towards a new fragmentation into closed economic blocs and spheres of influence. The European Union is a new kind of polity because its basis is the pooling of sovereignty and the establishment of common policies through negotiation. By developing its own common policies Europe creates an alternative to the present assumptions of global governance which emanate from Washington, and in doing so it has the potential to help prise open the closed political spaces of the global economy, such as the World Trade Organisation, the World Bank and the IMF, and to promote debates about key global issues such as poverty and environmental destruction.

International politics is shaped not only by ideas and ideals but also crucially by interests and power. If social democratic values are to influence the way the global economy is governed, then this is much more likely to be achieved if Europe has developed sufficient cohesion and unity so that it can speak with one voice, and use its economic weight for the discussion of alternative policies and institutions. The American monopoly is not healthy for the world or for America. This is why the advent of the euro can be regarded by social democrats with cautious optimism. It does not by itself signal solutions to the problems which confront us, but it is a sign that Europe is becoming more cohesive and more able to develop a common political will, although not in a manner which is either threatening or destabilising. It can provide alternative thinking and alternative leadership for the global economy by pioneering a new kind of democratic region-alism, more open and inclusive than what is on offer from Washington, and therefore more likely to be a stepping stone to the transnational forms of democratic governance which are so urgently required.

A trade union Europe

The euro will also provide opportunities for strengthening social movements, associations and networks within the European Union. European social networks on poverty, the environment, women's rights and many more will find it easier to operate the more Europe becomes a common space.

Trade unions in particular have much to gain from the euro. The Common Market was once viewed on the British left, and particularly amongst trade unionists, as little more than a capitalist club whose rules were rigged to favour the operations of capital against labour. These attitudes have mostly been abandoned, in part because the hammer blows of the Thatcher regime against the unions in Britain awakened them to the advantages of the legal protection of workers' rights which their counterparts enjoyed in most other states in the EU. Despite frequent protestations of internationalism, national ways of thinking had become ingrained in the British labour movement and it has taken time to shake off its belief that its political and industrial objectives should be pursued primarily at national level. But that change has been gathering pace in the last twenty years, and British trade unions now understand better the opportunities that Europe offers. The commitment to common standards of employment protection and workers' rights was embodied in the Social Chapter of the Maastricht Treaty. Britain's optout was one of the first things reversed by the Labour Government elected in 1997. The EU has set a number of important standards in labour rights which have gradually been incorporated into the UK, including equal pay for women, rights for part-time and short-term workers, rights for workers when companies are taken over, parental leave and maternity rights, maximum working times and minimum rest periods, and improved annual leave.

Capital has never suffered from the same disadvantages as labour in the global economy. It was supposed to be the workers by hand and brain who had no country, but that has become more true of capital, which has always understood the importance of operating around the whole world and in many jurisdictions, not just in the one from which it happens to originate. For a long period in the twentieth century this was not important, since the global economy was fragmented, and national economic sovereignty was enhanced. National regimes promoted particular accommodations between labour and capital, resting on employment protection, welfare programmes and the commitment to full employment.

Many of these institutions and policies are still in place, but in the last thirty years there has been significant opening of all national economies, and new forms of trade, production and communication. Capital, in the form of the modern transnational company, has been much quicker to take advantage of this situation than labour. It has displayed the flexibility and mobility which has always been at the heart of the dynamism of capitalism. Providing a countervailing power to capital has become increasingly hard for labour, yet the opportunity to become as transnational as capital has proved very difficult, not least because of so many separate national jurisdictions.

The euro can hardly by itself be expected to even matters up between labour and capital. But again the symbolic and practical effects of its introduction are important. British and European trade unions have come to recognise the advantages of pooling sovereignty. The euro could help make trade unions more effective by assisting the development of co-operation between unions within the EU, through more joint campaigns and exchange of information, and even trade union mergers. The euro will help bring home to everybody how the EU has developed into a common economic space with common rules. It is a jurisdiction in its own right which sits alongside, overlaps, and in some areas overrides that of the nation-state. It makes it easier to operate within this space, conceiving traditional trade union issues in a European rather than simply a national framework.

Trends towards greater union co-operation in Europe were already there before the euro, but the euro gives them added thrust, because it makes pay and prices more transparent within the eurozone than they have ever been. A common currency provides a common standard by which all activities can be compared. Different rates of pay in different branches of the same company in different countries, or in different parts of the same industry, are immediately exposed, in a way that was much less obvious before. The same degree of transparency that is found in existing common currency areas like the United Kingdom or Germany is now experienced for the first time across the whole of the EU. Mere awareness of differences does not of course mean that they wither away, but it directs attention to the causes of those differences, and it provides trade unions with powerful arguments for defending the interests of employees. Above all it encourages a much wider understanding of the global and transnational forces which shape our lives, and the most appropriate means for resisting or influencing them. In this way it encourages unions to think about policy and regulatory standards, and to challenge the 'common-sense' which neo-liberalism offers. Although neo-liberal ideas have tended to dominate some aspects of European integration in the last thirty years, particularly the single market and Economic and Monetary Union, their ascendancy is not immutable, and the creation of the eurozone will give a spur to those who want to develop the democratic potential of the Union and create institutions and forms of association that can regulate the European economy more effectively.

A citizens' Europe

By stimulating the organisation of social movements and networks, the euro will also help bring about the development of a European civil society, a Europe of citizens, rather than a Europe of states and elites. This is not exclusive to Europe; it is part of a wider change, the emergence of a vibrant transnational civil society and a new cosmopolitanism covering the whole world. In this process, the European Union is a crucial building bloc. It can be so precisely to the extent that it is not a new centralised nation-state or great power, but is rather a new form of association and co-operation, the kind of political space therefore which fosters and is defined by the multiple and overlapping identities of its citizens. From this standpoint, which is part of a much older progressive republican tradition of cosmopolitanism and internationalism, the significance of European integration is that it allows a partial escape from nationalism and the nation-state by promoting a common identity which does not supplant the separate national identities but exists in addition to them, and helps defuse some of their most negative and destructive consequences.

The euro can help promote this kind of cosmopolitan citizenship because it is not the currency imposed by a sovereign state, but has come about through the pooling of sovereignty. This is puzzling to state-centric theorists of right and left who assume that the present EU is an unstable equilibrium, and must sooner or later become either a fully-fledged state, suppressing all subordinate authority in the process, or must relapse back into separate component nation-states. But once we accept that the EU is a new kind of polity, rather than a transitional regime, European identity and citizenship can be detached from EU state forms and can be associated instead with the character of European civil society. The euro can be expected to play an important role in the development of this civil society and therefore to the development of the sense that Europe is something to which everyone within the European Union belongs. This can occur without the need for allegiance to a supranational state, with its emblems and rituals and offices.

One of the main attractions of the European Union is therefore that it is not a conventional state but a new identity which reflects the shared purposes and values of its citizens rather than its elites. Many critics of the European Union argue that up to now it has more often than not been the opposite—a union for the elites rather than for citizens. Why should the euro change that?

After all it was designed by the elites and imposed on the peoples of Europe, in most cases without a referendum and in the face of opinion polls in several countries, including Germany, which showed a majority rejecting it. But this has changed. Now that the euro has arrived opinion has moved strongly in favour of it; it has become a vital medium of exchange and communication, and a standard of value throughout the Union. By helping its citizens to see the European space more clearly it will encourage them to participate as Europeans in this space, and to recognise that one of their many identities is as a European, a citizen of the Union. It provides an everyday, taken-for-granted form of identity which will be much more effective than the flags and grand symbolic gestures which have so far characterised the rather unsuccessful attempts to promote a distinctive European identity.

If democracy is to survive at the national level it needs to be sustained by new democratic institutions and agencies that reach beyond the nation-state. The decline of corporatism has made the conduct of economic management more remote from citizens. The euro can help create new public awareness and public involvement in economic policy-making. It can encourage a move beyond the narrow conception of legal citizenship embodied in the Maastricht Treaty towards the achievement of broader social and economic rights for all European citizens. It can also lead to European citizens using the public spaces of Europe to raise issues of global social justice. In these ways, the euro can assist the emergence of Europe as a civil society which fosters a wider cosmopolitan citizenship in addition to national citizenship.

Conclusion

A European civil society is only part of the broader transnational civil society that is emerging, but it is an important part. Learning how to belong to several communities and being comfortable with the presence of multiple identities and multiple loyalties in our societies is crucial to all forms of democracy, and especially to social democracy. The idea that social democracy can be constructed in a closed national or local community no longer makes sense. The United Kingdom itself has been a prolonged experiment in building a multi-national state and therefore tolerating multiple identities for its citizens—English, Irish, Welsh, Scottish identities have been combined with local identities on the one hand and British identity on the other. Into this melting pot have come citizens bearing many other identities. Some of the traditional conflicts of identity within these islands, most notably that between the Irish and the English have become noticeably easier to handle through the emergence of the new common identity beyond both Britain and Ireland in the shape of the European Union.

One of the most important symbols of Britishness was the single currency, the pound sterling, which was adopted, with some concessions to Scotland, throughout the British jurisdiction. In the nineteenth century the pound sterling, because of the leading position of the British economy, became accepted as an international currency, backed by the gold standard, and was considered as good as gold. The price level at the start of the First World War in 1914 was slightly lower than it had been at the Battle of Waterloo a hundred years earlier. This stability of the currency underpinned not just the British Union but the wider British role in the world expressed particularly through its informal empire of trade as much as its formal empire of territory. The decline of British power in the twentieth century was associated with the decline in its currency, so much so that the succession of debilitating sterling crises from September 1931 when Britain was forced off the gold standard to Black Wednesday in September 1993 when Britain was forced out of the Exchange Rate Mechanism became occasions for national self-abasement and alarm.

What is true of almost every major sterling crisis until Black Wednesday is that they occurred when Labour Governments were in office, and were widely blamed on Labour's economic incompetence and profligate spending plans which could not be afforded or financed. Britain's experience was by no means unique. Social democratic governments in many countries have found it hard to reconcile their public spending commitments with the policies for macroeconomic stability required by the financial markets. One of the attractions of the euro therefore has been that the eurozone would be much less vulnerable to speculative attack, and better able to pursue policies of high investment, because it would be more insulated from the financial markets.

Britain's recent macro-economic success is frequently offered as the reason why Britain should not join the euro now or ever. Yet it is interesting that so many other European countries with a better long-term record in combining growth and welfare than Britain have been prepared to lock themselves into the euro, believing that it offers them still better opportunities to combine high levels of both in the future. The willingness of so many states of the Union to embrace the euro signals their determination to deepen their co-operation. Britain has a choice: helping to shape these developments from within the all-important early stages, strengthening social democratic Europe in the process; or remaining isolated, with diminishing influence on the outside. If Britain decides at a much later stage, in ten or twenty years time, that it should join the euro, it will also have to accept all the new institutions and policies which will have been developed to assist in managing the eurozone, but it will have played no part in shaping them.

That would be a disadvantage, but worse would be the brake which exclusion from the euro would mean on Britain's full participation in the next phase of European integration; ensuring the enlargement of the Union to the east, formulating a new constitutional framework for Europe; developing new regulatory capacities at the European level to counter global inequality and to limit environmental damage; to breathe fresh life into trade unions and voluntary associations; and to foster new forms of identity, community and citizenship. The euro does not guarantee any of these things. But if it helps us even a few steps along the way, it is worth embracing.

66

2 | Against Janet Bush and Larry Elliott

I f we—eurosceptics of the left—dare to take issue with the monetarist economics of the European single currency, we are told that we are political has-beens or members of the awkward squad who have failed to move with the times. If we mention our fears that membership of Economic and Monetary Union—by taking away our control not only over our currency and interest rates but also over public spending, borrowing and taxation—breaks the democratic link between voters and government, we are dismissed as unwitting foot soldiers for the xenophobic right. If we question the desire among Europe's political elites for some form of European state, without the necessary democratic institutions and structures that will allow Europe's peoples to hold their political masters to account, we are dismissed as anti-European.

This is as astonishing as it is depressing. The left of centre case against the euro has never been stronger. Left of centre parties have traditionally been in favour of economic policies that promote jobs and growth, yet the eurozone has failed to tackle mass unemployment. Left of centre parties have traditionally campaigned for economic institutions that are open and democratic, yet monetary policy in the eurozone is now dictated by a central bank that is unelected, unaccountable and secretive. Left of centre parties have always been deeply suspicious of economic structures that give excessive power and influence to big business, yet one of the driving forces behind monetary union is that of multinational capital which relishes the prospect of using the single currency to dismantle European social democracy. And left of centre parties have always cherished democracy—yet Europe's political elites are striving to build a new, highly centralised political structure in Europe without the involvement, or desire, or even knowledge, of Europe's peoples.

The rise of the Brussels Consensus

As late as 1983, Labour campaigned not just against monetary union but also against membership of the European Economic Community itself. The case against joining was summed up neatly in Labour's programme, put together in the autumn of 1973 for the forthcoming election: 'We would reject any kind of international agreement which compelled us to accept increased unemployment for the sake of maintaining a fixed parity, as is required by current proposals for economic and monetary union.'

How times have changed. Far from recognising that the euro project is anathema to the long-held aims of the left, the current new Labour leadership has, as in so many other instances, debunked past policy with relish. In 1997, new Labour declared itself to be in favour of the euro in principle, putting itself at the forefront of the drive towards economic deregulation in Europe.

So what happened? First, because Thatcher opposed UK membership of the Exchange Rate Mechanism (ERM), the correct position for a party of the left had to be to support the ERM. Mrs Thatcher conducted a running battle with Jacques Delors—therefore it was sensible for a left of centre party to snuggle up to Brussels. Actually, Mrs Thatcher was quite right about the ERM. It was deflationary and destroyed jobs on a grand scale. But for supporters of monetary union on the left, that does not weigh in the balance against an emotional desire to stand for whatever Thatcher was against, regardless of the facts.

The second factor might be called the Brussels Consensus. In the same way as western leaders have unthinkingly embraced the Washington Consensus in which the International Monetary Fund imposed identikit free market blueprints on the developing world, now the establishment is in the grip of another fashionable political assumption. Before the Washington Consensus was demolished by the evidence of the economic devastation it exported, greed was good. Now Europe is good. Europe is the new internationalism. And everything Europe does, we must do too, whether good or bad.

The proponents of this view are small in number but powerful, dominating the Foreign Office and Number 10, if not the Treasury. Avowed Labour eurosceptics such as Robin Cook and Peter Hain—not to mention Neil Kinnock and Tony Blair—have been seduced.

Hugo Young, writing in The *Guardian* on 16th March 2000, said that there were only two ways to persuade the British people to be more pro-European: seduction and terror. He concluded: 'In the time-scale Blair is thinking of, Britain will not love Europe … when the day of judgement comes, fear must stalk the land.'

The anti-democratic nature of the euro project is increasingly evident to the broad coalition gathered together under the banner of the anti-globalisation movement. This coalition recognises monetary union as part of a long European tradition, stretching back to the Enlightenment in the 18th century, of intellectuals and men and women of good intentions coming up with blueprints for progress and then forcing them on unwilling populations. The tendency towards a mild form of tyranny has been evident in the reaction of Europe's elite first to the Danish referendum on the euro and then the Irish referendum on the Nice treaty. Instead of accepting that the people had spoken, the reaction was simple: the people may have spoken but we know best and want a different answer; so the people had better think again.

Even if it could be proved that monetary union had delivered perfect economic outcomes, we would be wary of the euro's democratic failings. Falling voter turnout in elections is a reaction to the feeling that power has been sucked away from electorates and concentrated at the centre. The European Union seemed genuinely surprised at the riots on the streets of Gothenburg. It should not have been. Monetary union can be seen as the last gasp of the top-down modernist era that has been abandoned in virtually every other area of policy since the 1960s.

This by-pass of grass-roots opinion is now even more serious because it looks as if the rational economic underpinnings of Labour's euro policy are being abandoned. In October 1997, Tony Blair and Gordon Brown set five economic tests that have to be met 'clearly and unambiguously' and have stressed their importance repeatedly since. But in autumn 2001, Tony Blair linked his wish to go into the euro with the need to stand shoulder to shoulder with our partners in Europe against terrorism. At a stroke, the serious economic arguments against the euro were marginalised.

The change of tack is hardly surprising. As time has gone on, the economic arguments have moved decisively against those who advocate UK membership of the euro. It hardly helps the cause of Britain's euro-advocates that Germany has unemployment of 4.3 million and rising, and that the European Commission chose this particularly difficult time for the German people to rebuke their government for running a budget deficit just below the wholly arbitrary limit of 3 per cent of GDP imposed by the Growth and Stability Pact. Nor does it endear the British electorate to the euro for Gordon Brown to be told in January 2002 that, if we joined, he would have to cut public spending by anything between £10 billion (the Treasury's interpretation of the Commission's ruling) or £22 billion (the estimate published by the National Institute for Economic and Social Research) to come into line with the eurozone's fiscal rules.

An overarching motivation for the architects of the euro, one acknowledged and described by Andrew Gamble, is that substantial powers would have to be passed from Europe's nation states to supranational institutions in order to make the euro work—not only monetary policy (the exchange rate and interest rates) but also fiscal policy (taxation and public spending). In February 2002, Gerhard Schröder, the German Chancellor, spoke for the European establishment when he called for the 'Europeanisation' of 'everything to do with economic and financial policy.' He then made the link between economics and politics: 'European Monetary Union has to be complemented with political union—that was always the presumption of Europeans.' Acknowledging misgivings among the British electorate about the euro's political underpinnings, the German Chancellor suggested that the real destination would have to be described in different language: 'In this area, we need much more—let's call it co-ordination and co-operation to soothe British feelings—than before.'[1]

Euphemism is the stock in trade of those who see the euro as a stepping-stone towards some form of pan-European political entity—quite plainly described by the German Chancellor as a political union. Examples abound in Andrew Gamble's case for the single currency; we are offered, variously, a description of a post-EMU Europe as a 'new form of political authority', a 'post-national' EU, and even a 'cosmopolitan citizenship'.

The Brussels Consensus is on the march. Now, surely, is the time for the Labour movement to display its long tradition of independent thought and force the Government to get back to the bread and butter issues of jobs and democracy that have always been at the heart of suspicions about the euro project.

We make no apology for examining the economics of the euro in depth. To do otherwise would be dangerous. Nobody with even a rudimentary knowledge of history can disagree that bad economics leads to bad politics. Mass unemployment has on too many occasions been the breeding ground for discontented nationalism and social unrest, not least in Germany in the 1930s and in some of the disappointed and disaffected Middle Eastern economies of today. Economic prosperity has been the bedrock of all vibrant post-war western democracies, none more so than Germany.

As Ed Balls, Chief Economic Advisor to the Treasury, said in a speech in February 2002: 'Too often over the last 100 years we have had decisions made with a political imperative overriding economic reasons ... Most governments lose power because they fail on the economy. If you want to get your politics right you have got to get the economics right. If you make a political decision when the economics is not right the economic and political consequences can be very damaging.' He usefully reminded us that Britain's decision to join the ERM some 10 years ago—supported by the Labour Party—was bad economics, made for political reasons. The result was a doubling of unemployment, 1.75 million households in negative equity, 100,000 businesses bankrupt and the destruction of a government.

Andrew Gamble subjugates economics to 'political choice'. He starts from an aspiration to build a European political entity and then works backwards. What will make people feel European? What will be the spur to the creation of the new European political space? His answer is the euro—precisely because, in its current form, it is unworkable. The EU's ability to develop new policies, such as a larger EU budget, will be the crucial test for its ability to make the euro work. New policies and institutional arrangements will become a practical necessity. The euro, Gamble argues, 'forces into the open questions about the constitutional architecture of Europe and makes it much harder for these to be avoided in the way they often have been up to now'.

He is not alone in this thought. In an interview with The *Financial Times* on 4th December 2001, Romano Prodi, President of the European Commission, said: 'I am sure the euro will oblige us to introduce a new set of economic policy instruments. It is politically impossible to propose that now. But some day there will be a crisis and new instruments will be created.'

We are entitled to ask how much unemployment is a price worth paying for the successful creation of a European 'political space'. Clearly, the current level of 10 per cent is not enough to force Europeans into accepting a new political identity. Will unemployment of 20 per cent be enough? And who will decide how much pain the ordinary working people of Europe should be expected to take? Europe's elites, of course, men and women who have secure jobs and generous salaries who, at no risk to their own well-being, are itching to throw the dice and gamble with people's futures.

The euro's economic failures

Nearly three years on from the launch of the euro, much of what the Labour movement feared in the 1970s and continues to fear now has come to pass. One of the euro lobby's most consistent claims since the euro was launched in January 1999 is that Britain's economy would suffer by staying outside of monetary union, that Britain is too small to go it alone, that we would lose millions of jobs unless we joined and that inward investment would dry up.

This scare-mongering has become less believable as people realise that economic meltdown has not materialised. Given the peculiar British propensity towards pessimism about our post-war performance, it may be difficult to believe that Britain has outperformed the continental economies for quite some years now.

The ultimate yardstick of economic success or failure is whether an economic system creates jobs. Bill Morris of the TGWU puts jobs at the centre of his judgement on the euro: 'I do not deny the resonance of issues of national sovereignty and democracy which are also raised by the move towards a common currency, but I believe that for the trade union movement, they are largely considered in terms of their impact on the prospects for the economy and employment.'[2]

The eurozone's performance on jobs has been awful. In 1999, when the euro was launched, the average unemployment rate for the 11 countries that joined was 10.5 per cent. By August 2001, with the help of a huge devaluation in the euro, it had fallen to 8.3 per cent but then started rising again. The euro has not acted as a motor for job creation. In contrast, Britain's unemployment rate has been far lower than the eurozone average for the entire period since the euro was launched, falling from 6.3 per cent in 1999 to 5.1 per cent recently.

UK manufacturing, even with the difficulties of a weak euro against the pound, has done far better than eurozone manufacturing. Since 1992 (when Britain left the ERM but continental economies were squeezing themselves to meet the entry requirements for EMU), Germany has lost nearly one in five of its manufacturing jobs and France one in 10. Britain too has lost manufacturing jobs but only one in 15.

Britain's far superior record on jobs has come at the same time as having lower inflation and attracting more foreign investment over each of the past five years than Germany, France, Italy, the Netherlands, Belgium and Luxembourg put together. No wonder the euro has been chronically weak against the pound. Can we really argue yet that the euro and the eurozone economy is a success and that we, in a far stronger position, should join?

Institutionalised deflation

The reason for Europe's inability to tackle mass unemployment is obvious. It is that Economic and Monetary Union, enshrined in the Maastricht Treaty, is institutionalised deflation. There is, quite simply, no mechanism in the design of EMU aimed at promoting jobs. The architects and now managers of the euro are orthodox monetarists and fiscal Puritans. The result is that euro-zone interest rates are set too high and budgets are too restricted, leading to low growth and mass unemployment.

Having endured the monetarist experiment of Thatcherism, is this really what we in Britain want? Do we want to join a system that would prevent Gordon Brown from carrying through his election promise of raising investment—so long overdue and so sorely needed—in public services? One of the reasons that conti-nental economies are still looked at by many in this country with envy is that, over the years, they have chosen to spend more of their respective national incomes on public services. Now, just when British has built up a strong economy that allows us, for the first time since the war, to outspend France and Germany on public services, is this really the time to throw away our big chance?

The threat has rarely been as well put as by Peter Hain, former sceptic, now a fully paid up member of the Brussels Consensus. Writing in 1995, he said: 'Today, Europe is imperilled, not by the issues which excite chauvinist fantasies in the British right, but by its self-imposed monetarist straitjacket and its preoccupation with free market competition. Instead of full employment, growth, investment and redistribution being the overriding goals of European economic policy, price, currency and interest rate stability are being pursued to an obsessive degree, together with tight restrictions on public spending, public borrowing and public debt.'[3]

Maastricht was drafted in an era when inflation was regarded as the biggest threat to world economic prosperity and in deference to the wishes of Germany which was prepared to sacrifice its tried and trusted currency, the Deutschemark, in exchange for becoming accepted once and for all as a political equal in the family of modern European democracies. The absolute independence of the European Central Bank—and its sole mandate to bear down on inflation—was the price of Germany's membership of EMU.

The truth is that deflation, rather than inflation, is the problem facing the global economy in the 21st century. Japan, the world's second largest economy, is already struggling with the difficulty of deflation, and the ECB seems intent on pushing the eurozone economy in the same direction. The Maastricht Treaty has cast a long shadow over European economies for many years before the euro was launched. In the 1980s and 1990s, European governments pursued deflationary economic policies on a long march towards membership. Candidate economies bore down on inflation and budget deficits at the same time to meet the Treaty's convergence criteria, a process that has left a lasting legacy of mass unemployment. Brian Burkitt at Bradford University estimates that, if Britain had gone down this route too, it would have had to cut public spending or raise taxes by £42 billion.

Since the euro's launch, the straitjacket has been kept as tight as ever. The ECB has followed its anti-inflationary mandate with zeal. While the Bank of England has cut interest rates seven times, the ECB has cut only four times—and then with glacial speed—and unemployment in the eurozone is heading for double digits once more.

The pro-euro lobby argues that both banks are independent and therefore that the ECB is no bar to joining the euro. But the degree of independence is quite different. The Bank of England is formally accountable to the UK Chancellor of the Exchequer and to Parliament, and regularly has to account for its behaviour and record. The ECB, by contrast, is unaccountable by treaty. Pro-euro campaigners say that, inside the euro, Britain would have a voice on the ECB that would promote British interests. This is simply not true. Article 107 of the Amended Treaty of Rome forbids members of the ECB to be influenced in any way by the needs of their home nations: 'When exercising the powers and carrying out the tasks and duties conferred upon them by this Treaty and the Statute of the European System of Central Banks (ESCB), neither the ECB, nor a national central bank, nor any member of their decision making bodies shall seek or take instructions from Community institutions or bodies, from any government of a Member State or from any other body. The Community institutions and bodies and the governments of the Member States undertake to respect this principle and not to seek to influence the members of the decision making bodies of the ECB or of the national central banks in the performance of their tasks.'

Even if the ECB was the best run central bank in the world, it would still have the impossible task of setting a single interest rate that was right for 12 or more economies and 320 million people. What rate is right for Germany, whose growth is stagnating and unemployment on the rise again, as well as the Netherlands whose inflation rate is soaring? Living with a single interest rate—in a one-size-fits-all system, as this is often described—is deeply uncomfortable if not impossible without both economic convergence and flexibility, both of which are sorely lacking.

The traditional way out of a monetary straitjacket is the flexible use of fiscal policy. Instead, Eurozone politicians have opted for a fiscal straitjacket to complement the deflationary tendency of the ECB. The Growth and Stability Pact imposes a strict 3 per cent limit on budget deficits at all times, even in recession, and operates a system of penalties for countries going above the limit —usually because of recession. So far from allowing governments leeway to run deficits to help cushion economic downturns—as is quite usual in traditional economic management—it actually requires governments to cut public spending or raise taxes when their economies are in the worst trouble.

The rigidity of the eurozone's fiscal framework has already had sweeping effects, all too familiar to Britain after the Thatcher years, in continental economies. In order to take public spending off the balance sheet, Public Finance Initiatives and straight privatisation have grown exponentially. Welfare systems across Europe—so often cited as a reason why Britain should join the euro—are being squeezed. Now, with the first world economic slowdown since the euro was launched underway, this process is accelerating. In November, the German Finance Minister announced a programme of privatisations to bring the Government's budget deficit within the limits of the Pact. The previous month, emergency privatisation measures in Italy and France (public owned real estate and a motorway company respectively) were announced for the same reason.

Fundamental design flaws

Even if the ECB's mandate were to be changed and even if the Growth and Stability Pact were to be loosened, monetary union would still be far too inflexible to promote jobs and prosperity. Monetary unions take away the flexibility over economic policy normally enjoyed by national governments. Different forms of flexibility have to be found to compensate for this; otherwise permanent strains can develop with no way of righting imbalances between prospering and stagnating regions.

One source of flexibility is the mobility of labour so that people can move freely around a single currency zone to look for work and so iron out differences between high unemployment and low unemployment regions. The fact is, however, that mobility in the EU is six times less than in America where people regularly up-sticks to find work.

Another, even more important factor is the existence of an 'automatic stabiliser' in the form of fiscal transfers that move money from prospering regions to under-performing ones. No monetary union has ever worked without these transfers, whether it is the union between western and eastern Germany post-reunification or the union between the Czech Republic and Slovakia, the union formed between northern and southern Italy or indeed the union between England and Scotland.

We do not believe that EMU will work well—and may not even survive in the long-term—without a further transfer of political power to the EU so that taxes can be raised centrally and provide for the necessary fiscal transfers. At present, the EU's budget is only 1.27 per cent of total GDP. In America, 25 per cent or more of US GDP is available for transfers. This, above all, has ensured that the American monetary union has been a success.

Andrew Gamble agrees with this analysis but fails to acknowledge the rather irritating fact that there is no political backing for a large, centralised budget. Proposals from the Commission and Belgium in mid-2001 for a new EU tax (actually involving no new money) was immediately slapped down by Member States who know that electorates do not want to pay any more for the running of the EU. Gerrit Zalm, the Dutch Finance Minister, said: 'The last time a new tax was launched in The Netherlands it resulted in the Eighty Years War. I am not sure a new tax for the EU would be much better this time.'

This episode graphically revealed the hole in the middle of the euro project. It needs a federal budget and a significant degree of economic and political centralisation to work but there is no appetite for this among Europe's electorates.

Ed Balls highlighted precisely this point in his 1992 Fabian Society pamphlet: 'The mistake is to let economic schemes run ahead of political realities. The goal of a single European currency, like an ever closer union, is not inherently misconceived. But to work, it requires a much closer degree of social and political cohesion and integration than Europe is likely to achieve in this decade and probably the next too.'[4]

The euro: battering ram to the free market in Europe

In the absence of either labour mobility or an automatic stabiliser, the managers of the euro are relying on finding flexibility through another route that is anathema to the left: labour market flexibility. Take away the jargon and this means dismantling trade union protections, giving employers the freedom to hire and fire and to remove, as far as possible, employment and social protection that, employers argue, raise the cost of employing labour. This is dismaying, particularly for the pro-euro left—even ignoring the uncomfortable truth that new Labour is the EU's most passionate advocate of deregulation.

Campaigners for the euro on the British left have partly based their support for membership on a dreadful misunderstanding. They have always seen the euro as a passport out of the desert of free market Thatcherite economics into the promised land of European social and labour solidarity. They could not be more wrong.

Firstly, they have wrongly conflated membership of the EU and membership of the euro. After the scorched earth Thatcher years, Tony Blair signed up to the Social Chapter and other EU social policies because he believed in them. He did not need Britain to be in the euro to embrace EU legislation. Secondly, the economics of the euro require deregulation in the absence of the other elements—most notably fiscal federalism—described above. EMU will entrench liberal economics in Europe.

The clearest description of this dynamic comes from Dr Otmar Issing, Chief Economist of the ECB. He said: 'The dangers (of lack of free market reform) can be identified relatively easily. The most obvious one is the lack of flexibility in the labour market. In conjunction with the high initial level of unemployment at the start of monetary union, this poses an almost lethal threat to monetary union.'

Even more pertinent for those on the pro-euro left who are looking to the euro for a guarantee of higher social standards, Dr Issing wrote: 'Calls for a social union (seemingly backed by noble motives) to complement or correct monetary union (sometimes resented as "a Europe of money and finance") go in the wrong direction. If one were to concede to such demands, rising unemployment and mounting tensions between countries and regions would be the consequence. Eventually, the very survival of Monetary Union would be at risk.'[5]

The euro is, and was always intended to be, a battering ram towards the free market in Europe after decades when Europe held out against liberal economics. It is no accident that the most ardent advocates of EMU are multinational corporations who see the single currency as the means to secure a single European state in which capital roams free and labour is cheap, plentiful and less protected. Feather bedding European big business may be a reason for supporting the euro. It is not one for the left of centre.

Entrenching globalisation

This defeatism—and that includes the handful of trade union leaders who have signed up for the pro-euro cause—appears to stem from a belief that no nation state can survive the ravages of a global economy on its own. By joining a large trading bloc with a single currency will give us the necessary protection. But there is no evidence that you can buy protection by joining together to form a bigger unit. The richest state in Asia is Singapore—a small island with almost no natural resources; the richest country in Europe is Switzerland, which is not even in the EU, never mind the euro. Neither is it the case that a free trade area or single market needs a single currency. Canada and Mexico are part of the North Atlantic Free Trade Area with America. Both have decided against adopting the dollar as a single currency.

In fact, none of the favourite economic arguments for the euro stand up to scrutiny. Joining the euro will not, for example, rid us of destabilising currency fluctuations. The eurozone accounts for 43 per cent of British trade. The dollar is, overall, more important to the British economy than is the euro. The pound is far more stable against the dollar than the pound is against the euro or the euro is against the dollar. Any currency stability for our trade with the eurozone would be balanced by increased volatility for our trade with the rest of the world.

The arguments that joining the euro will bring transparency of prices and remove transaction costs are similarly dubious. Even the pro-euro lobby does not rate these arguments. Alison Cottrell, a prominent pro-euro lobbyist, said: 'If the euro's primary purpose in life were to allow consumers in Hamburg to spot a bargain in Capri and avoid hefty conversion changes, the whole exercise would scarcely have been worth the effort. The internet, credit cards and competition policy could have produced most of the benefits with none of the upheaval.'[6]

It is perfectly obvious that the weakness of the economic case in favour of the euro is the reason why Tony Blair and his foot soldiers in the long march to euro membership have started ignoring the economic risks and concentrating on political arguments instead.

It's politics, stupid

We take serious issue with Andrew Gamble's hope that the euro, by its failings, will force political change but at least he is honest:

he has a political vision of Europe and offers an analysis of how to get there. The arguments of others in the pro-euro camp are less coherent, combining economic scare stories, cultural pro-Europeanism (laced with a whiff of anti-Americanism) and, perhaps above all, a concern not to be left out or left behind—the result of long decades of angst about Britain's post-war decline.

Rational thought is being replaced by political dream-making. Peter Hain calls his tour of the country to promote the euro 'patriotic'. Tony Blair says we have to go into the euro to build a new world order to fight terrorism. Even for those who broadly believe that Britain should join the euro this was a mysterious logical leap. What Tony Blair was really arguing for was multi-lateralism. His argument, in essence, appears to be that it a dangerous world out there and that no nation is strong enough to act alone. Britain needs to engage fully in Europe and, to do that, we must be in the euro. We disagree. Has Tony Blair lacked influence in Europe in the aftermath of 11th September? The scramble by European leaders for a dinner invitation to Number 10 to discuss the war on terrorism would suggest not.

Outside the euro, Britain has played a leading role both in Europe and in the wider world. It has been at the forefront, with France—Europe's other major military power—of efforts to build a common European defence policy and it has—to the chagrin of many on the left—led the effort to deregulate European markets and to complete the Single Market.

Britain's interests and assets are spread around the world. Much of its influence—in the Commonwealth, in relation to the United States—has nothing to do with its membership of the EU. Britain has a permanent seat on the UN Security Council and is a prominent member of NATO. Britain is the fourth largest economy in the world and, as a member of the Group of Eight industrialised countries, highly influential in global economic affairs.

Far from losing influence by remaining outside the euro, we believe Britain's power would be diminished inside. As part of the process of economic and political centralisation of the euro-zone, the EU is already seeking to replace national representation on both the Security Council and the G8 with EU representation. Even more pertinently, inside the euro, Britain's economic interests would be represented by a single vote in the ECB—a vote, as we have seen, that would not be allowed to take any account of British considerations. Britain's influence in its economic affairs is surely far more powerful by retaining the Bank of England whose job it is exclusively to look after British economic interests. Andrew Gamble says that our self-government will be enhanced by giving away control over economic policy. How so? The meaning of self-government surely brooks no ambiguity. Surely it means governing ourselves?

Britain already has a well-established multilateral dimension through our membership of the EU. This is quite distinct from membership of the euro. Conflating membership of the EU with membership of the single currency is misleading. It is perfectly possible to support UK membership of the EU whilst being opposed to joining the euro.

The other political motivation of the pro-euro lobby is empire building. Tony Blair has made it clear he wants to help Europe become a superpower. This has traditional resonance on the left who have long desired to see a social democratic, European power to challenge the hegemony of America with its neo-liberal economics and foreign adventurism.

The euro is widely seen in Europe as a catalyst to progress towards ever closer union and a European superpower. In economic terms, the euro would challenge the supremacy of the dollar as the world's reserve currency, a particular interest of the French political classes. In political terms, it would provide, as we have seen, the spur to European centralisation.

The centralisation of power in Europe may not, in itself, necessarily a bad thing. There are many people who are sceptical about the way EMU has been designed who would nevertheless, in the longer-term, like to see some kind of federal European state. But what kind of state or superpower will it be, on current evidence? Will it, as we fear, move away from the social economic model because of the deficiencies evident in the construction of EMU? Will the club be inclusive or exclusive? The EU has certainly shown worrying leanings towards the latter in its negotiations with those countries from central and eastern Europe who want to join the Union.

The approach to negotiations about enlargement has shown all the hallmarks of a new imperialism that does not inspire confidence that Europe will fulfil its proper destiny of reuniting the continent after the Second World War and Cold War. Too often, the EU has been guilty of what President Aleksander Kwasniewski of Poland has called a 'virus of selfishness'. The EU has a high-handed attitude toward accession candidates. The negotiations have been entirely one-sided. Every accession country has to comply with the 40,000 items of the *acquis communautaire*, deregulate their economies, comply with Maastricht and sign up to all EU treaties, past and present, with no hope of opt-outs. The price of membership is extraordinarily high. But what they get in return is highly conditional. For example, because of the EU's failure to tackle reform of the Common Agricultural Policy (CAP), the accession countries are being told that they will not get access to the full array of agricultural subsidies. And, because of western discomfort with economic immigration, they will not be allowed free movement of labour—although westerners have carte blanche to move east.

Above all, will the European political entity that the political classes want to develop be democratic? Will the people of Europe be consulted about what they want? They have not been about the euro (with the notable exception of Denmark and potentially Britain and Sweden). As we have said, even if the euro were to produce perfect economic outcomes, we would still feel deeply uncomfortable if this was not allied to democracy. Singapore is a highly successful economy but most of us would not want to live with its autocratic political system.

What about democracy?

The left has always fought for democratic and accountable institutions. All of us believe in bringing power closer to people. It is one of the most extraordinary aspects of the Blair Government's advocacy of the euro that it has chosen to devolve power to Scotland, Wales, Northern Ireland and London but asserts that it has no constitutional or political concerns about transferring the power of the British government to a pooled sovereignty in Europe.

Andrew Gamble describes the United Kingdom as an experiment in building a multi-national state and therefore tolerating multiple identities for its citizens as an argument for the building of a European state, with or without the consent of its peoples. How extraordinary. Devolution, however partial, to Scotland and Wales was undertaken because these peoples wanted a democratic voice that more closely reflected both their concerns and their identity. The UK is closer to disintegrating than it has been for hundreds of years and quite rightly. It has embraced devolution, rebuilding nation states more closely to reflect the will of the peoples concerned.

We are not arguing for the nation state in perpetuity. But we do oppose dismantling it to sign up for something less democratic on the basis of an uncertain and dubious rationale. Nobody argues that Westminster politicians (or those at Holyrood or in Cardiff) are loved but at least they are, every four or five years, accountable to us. This is not yet the case with Europe. The idea of building a pan-European democracy is legitimate but only if there is a popular desire for such a thing. At the moment, it does not exist and it cannot until a European *demos* develops, a far off prospect.

As the debate in Britain about the euro gathers momentum—at least in Westminster circles—we should ask ourselves some simple questions. What is the role of politicians in a democracy? To represent and serve the people who elected them? Yes. To lead in times of war? Yes. To drive us into a political and economic experiment that does not interest us? No. Why is the status quo in Europe inadequate? Has the EU in its current form not already proved a spectacular success in fostering established democracies in Europe? Why do Europe's political classes now want to build some kind of European state? Is it just habit after decades of trying to push political integration? Can they not be weaned off their 1950s and 1960s agenda and into the modern world with its new set of problems?

Do we regularly fail to vote at European elections because the European state is not centralised enough? Or is it because the European state is already too remote to secure our interest and participation? And why, if the political aspirations of Europe's political elites are so exciting, do they not share them with us instead of pursuing them with such a level of secrecy, such obscurantist language and with no offer of a popular vote on these profound matters?

A positive future outside the euro

It has often been said that the organic, reflective, richly muddled political culture of Britain, in which policy is generally made with the people's views in mind, has been the core reason why Britain has enjoyed centuries of relative political stability. A decision to join the euro in the face of popular opposition is an aberration from Britain's relatively settled political history.

We do not believe that forcing grand political schemes on scep-tical or simply disinterested electorates is a recipe for future social cohesion; quite the opposite. We not only believe that the euro is bad economics, for Britain and our European partners, but also that it fails the overriding, critical test of democracy. And we believe that we, the people, have the power—and the argu-ments—to say no.

Surely there must be a better way and it is the left that should be enunciating it. So many friends on the left share our concerns about the euro but cannot bear to put the arguments because they do not want to be bracketed with Tories. This really is not good enough. It is true that the right has nothing positive to say about Britain's future in Europe but that makes it even more important for we on the left to move the euro debate away from Queen, country and a thousand years of history and start talking about jobs and democracy.

Others on the left are sceptical but are resigned to the euro because it is inevitable. Why is there such defeatism about the euro and such courage elsewhere? We think that the IMF is spreading a particularly virulent form of free market capitalism and we challenge it. The same goes for the WTO and the immorality of demanding debt repayments from the poorest people in the world. We could have invoked the myth of inevitability about free trade and debt but we chose not to.

The left should start by demanding root and branch reform of the European Central Bank, in co-operation with like-minded colleagues across Europe. The left should lead the debate on breaking the austerity psychology on budgets and be demanding policies to tackle mass unemployment.

We should be campaigning for accession countries in central and eastern Europe to be put on a fast track to EU membership with the onerous conditions of entry scaled back. We should reject the imposition on these countries of a monetarist dogma that will hold back their development. We should demand more democracy in the EU institutions and reject the notion, propagated by the British pro-euro lobby among others, that in order to be a good European, we have to accept every dot and comma of every treaty, every inter-governmental conference and every directive, whether good or bad.

The left should be campaigning for a decentralised Europe. Why demand devolution at home but concede to the accretion of power at the centre in Europe? We should be rejecting the harmonisation and homogenisation of politics in the EU and demanding a flexible Europe with a multiplicity of independent voices which could contribute to a far more dynamic European polity. The current, unaccountable, top-down, centralised model is not delivering. Everyone knows that the CAP is an abomination but nobody has been competent enough to reform it or scrap it. Until the European institutions prove that they are up to the job, we should demand that they do less but do it better.

Above all, we should question the blueprints offered to us by our political masters. After all, their grand project will not work without our consent and our enthusiasm.

References

1   The *Guardian*, 22nd February 2002

2   *The Single European Currency in National Perspective: A Community in Crisis?*, Bernard H Moss and Jonathan Michie (eds), Macmillan 1998

3   *Ayes to the left: A Future for Socialism*, Peter Hain, Lawrence & Wishart, 1995

4   *Euro-Monetarism—Why Britain was ensnared and how it should escape*, Edward Balls, Fabian Society, December 1992

5   From a lecture given on 20th September 1999 in Frankfurt on the occasion of the 50th Anniversary of *Frankfurter Allegmeine*. Published in March 2000 in *IEA Journal*

6   *Independent on Sunday*, 2nd September 2001

Paying for Progress
A New Politics of Tax for Public Spending

The Commission on Taxation and Citizenship

Taxation—and the public spending it pays for—is the subject of the fiercest political controversy. *Paying for Progress: A New Politics of Tax* for Public Spending offers a compelling new approach.

Reporting the results of new research into public attitudes towards taxation, Paying for Progress argues that the public must be 'reconnected' to the taxes they pay and the public services which these finance. To do this it proposes the greater use of 'earmarked' taxes, including a new tax to fund the National Health Service. Setting out a new philosophy of citzenship to underpin taxation policy, it recommends a series of reforms to meet the goals of social inclusion and environmental protection. And it asks: are higher taxes needed to pay for public services?

Written in a lively and accessible style for the general reader, *Paying for Progress* makes an important contribution to political thought and policy in the first decade of the 21st century. Providing key information on the UK tax system, it will also be an invaluable text for students and researchers in politics, economics, public administration, law and accountancy.

'Coherent, radical and lucid... this important book raises critical questions for the future of British politics'
Will Hutton, Chief Executive, the Industrial Society

'Highly recommended... The clarity with which it explores the facts and arguments about the tax system make it an extremely valuable text for students and researchers... it will provide a benchmark for future work on taxation reform'
Andrew Gamble, Professor of Politics, University of Sheffield

November 2000 ■ ISBN 07163 6003 9 ■ £9.95

Other Fabian Society Publications

Coping with Post-democracy

Colin Crouch

'In this stimulating new pamphlet, Professor Colin Crouch makes links between the decline of the state and the waning of democratic enthusiasm. When so much of the public sector has been handed over to private operators, Crouch argues, what becomes of the image of government as a task that matters? If every public function is tested by its conformity with private-sector management goals, why should anyone get excited about choosing between parties? If government is routinely seen as incompetent, and the company as the only source of expertise, no wonder politics and democracy, in America if not yet here, are at an all-time low. This is a fate that Labour, not so long ago, would have been desperate to avoid ... At some stage, the Labour party may have to confront the lacuna that has been created on the left.'
Hugo Young, The *Guardian*

Colin Crouch is Professor of Sociology at the European University Institute, Florence, and External Scientific member of the Max Planck Institute for Society Research, Cologne

December 2000 ■ ISBN 07163 0598 4 ■ £6.95